BAD LEG

OR

NO BAD LEG

The life of
JAMES
DUPRE DEAL

In conversation with Rob Dunn

A hero is an ordinary individual who finds the strength to persevere and endure in spite of overwhelming obstacles.

Christopher Reeve

The only disability in life is a bad attitude

Scott Hamilton

Chapters

MY CHILDHOOD

1940 – 1951

. MY TEENAGE YEARS 1952 – 1959

THE BELLE VUE YEARS

1956 -1958

LIFE WITH MY DAD

1940 - 1959

MY FIRST MARRIAGE

1960 – 1963

LIFE WITH MY DAD

1960 - 2002

MY SECOND MARRIAGE

1977 – 2013

ALONE AGAIN

2013 -

MY NAME IS JAMES DUPRE DEAL.

I WAS BORN ON 22nd NOVEMBER 1940. AT NELL LANE HOSPITAL, WITHINGTON, MANCHESTER.

THEY TOLD

MUM AND DAD THAT I WOULDN'T SURVIVE BUT I DID SO NOW AFTER MANY, MANY, YEARS I WANT TO TELL YOU MY LIFE STORY AS I REMEMBER IT.

For reasons that will become apparent as his story unfolds, Jim was unable to write this story himself.

The story was compiled by Rob Dunn writing under the pseudonym Arjay Dee from tapes recorded by Jim and in many afternoons of conversation. Although the compilation and editing were not done by Jim, the story is written in the first person singular.

Chapter One

Childhood

1940-1951

I was born on the 22nd November 1940 in Nell Lane Hospital, Withington. Manchester. They told me Mum and Dad that I wouldn't survive but I did. So, after many, many, years I want to tell you my life story as I see it.

I became the oldest child in the family as I was to have two sisters and a brother younger than me. I survived after the Doctors telling my Mother that at 3 pounds eight ounces, I had very little chance. As a consequence, I spent my first weeks in hospital to recover.

My Mother told me, when the midwife, who was a strong and very big woman, first saw me in my cot at home, I surprised everyone. I took hold of her finger and wouldn't let go.

She said to my Mother

"This boy is going nowhere. He is a survivor. Those Doctors have got it all wrong.

I was born with a deformed leg and still have one leg shorter than the other. I have lived all my life with built up shoes. This made my life difficult but I have survived for seventy-eight years. Bad leg or no bad leg.

I think I was a disappointment to my Dad and I believe he never really liked me. He was a good Dad and I loved him very much but he never told me he loved me.

Editor's note.

When James Du Pre Deal was born in 1940, His Father, also James was 27, born on 19 May 1913 in Molash, Kent, his father, Samuel, was 31 and his mother, Sarah, was 32. He married Mary Roberts on 20 May 1939. They had four children in 14 years.

Mary had given birth to three children before 1940. A boy who had died early in infancy and a set of still born twins. It is not clear who the Father was, but assumed to be James Deal senior.

Nell Lane Hospital was a former Victorian workhouse and had been used a s military hospital during WW1 remaining as such until 1928 when it reverted to civilian use. Prior to the National Health Service in 1948. The

Chorlton Union Workhouse, Nell Lane, Withington was opened in 1855. The workhouse site also included the Chorlton Union Cemetery which served the Chorlton Union area as well the workhouse and hospital until it reached its capacity in 1920.

By 1948 it had become one of the largest general hospitals in the country and was established as the focal point for the hospitals of the newly-formed South Manchester Group under the overall control of the Manchester Regional Hospital Board.

My Family lived at 102 Sloane Street. Moss Side Manchester on the corner of Moss Lane East. It was a big house and we lived on the ground floor. Other families lived upstairs; I think they were Polish.

At the time I was born, my Mum and Dad shared the ground floor with a man I came to know as Uncle Jack, who was no relation but would be a major influence on my life. We had three bedrooms a kitchen and a parlour. No garden just a back yard for the shared toilet. At the back of the yard the alleyway ran down behind all the terraced houses on Sloane Street.

Editor's note

The Deal household is clearly seen at the junction with Moss Lane on the right-hand side of the street. Note that it is larger than other properties.

During the blitz of WW11, bombs fell as indicated

My Mum and Dad had met when they both used to go to the wrestling at Belle Vue. I am not sure whether they had to get married but I believe that they did that because my Mum was pregnant.

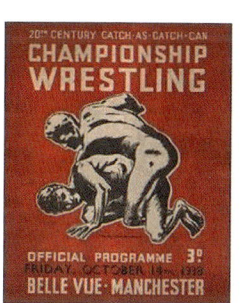

As will become apparent as my story unfolds, the wrestling would be a part of my life too in years to come, and so will Belle Vue.

Editor's Note.

> Belle Vue Zoological Gardens were originally meant to be an enjoyable pastime for the middle classes, however they very quickly became one of the North West's biggest attractions. At the height of Belle Vue's popularity it was host to around 2 million visitors a year. The site eventually became home to exotic animals, live music, dancing, speedway, boxing and wrestling, greyhound racing, football, rugby league and a myriad of other entertainments.
>
> Just about anyone who spent time in Manchester, prior to Belle Vue finally closing its doors in 1987, has a story to tell about it.

As I have said before, I didn't think my Dad liked me. He said

"You were more trouble than you were worth."

The problem was that not only was I born with a deformed leg, but also, I had meant a lot of hospital appointments.

I was very late in developing and by the age of two I had not been able to sit up and spent a lot of time lying in my cot or in my pram in the backyard.

Typical backyard

On one occasion, I was lucky to survive because whilst lying in my pram in the backyard, a dog, I was told it was a Yorkshire terrier, jumped in the pram. Grabbed hold of my right arm and dragged me out down the back alley. Fortunately, this was all heard and my Mum chased after the dog who left me there in the alleyway; I still have the three big scars on my right arm from the dog bite.

If the dog was indeed a Yorkshire terrier, then I must have been very small indeed for such a small dog to be able to do that.

The police were called and the dog was found and put down.

My lack of sitting had been worrying my Mum who asked the mid-wife what to do. She told my Mum

"Get some olive oil. Place him on your knee face down and rub the oil into the base of his spine."

Mum did this and in a few weeks, I was pulling myself, but could still not walk. When I did start to walk, my deformed left leg meant that I had to walk on tiptoe with my left foot not able to be placed on the floor.

You can imagine that walking like this was difficult and I would fall over a lot. Playing with other kids in the alleyway wasn't easy for me on those cobbles.

Remember one occasion, trying to run down the alley after it had been raining, and like kids run through a puddle, my leg went down a grid which had no top on it and I fell face down in the water. Got absolutely soaked.

When I got home, did I get any sympathy? No, I got a clip round the ear from my Mum and grounded for a few weeks.

In between having children, she worked in a public laundry and would wash clothes for people who didn't want to do that themselves. It was a small but helpful income for the family. My Mum was born in West Derby, Liverpool in 1919.

Her Mum, Sarah was eighteen when Mum was born but unfortunately, she died in the child birth. Her Dad, Ralph Roberts, couldn't look after her on his own so she was brought up in a children's home.

She never learned to read or write.

My Dad was a hard worker, I have to give him praise for that. Before WW11 he had started work in the kitchen at the Midland Hotel in central Manchester as a trainee chef, but. soon left to become a painter and decorator.

He joined the army in WW11 and was assigned to an antiaircraft battery and would later see service in North Africa. He was demobilised in 1946 and my sister Sylvia was born in 1947.

Uncle Jack lived with us throughout my childhood. His real name was John Du Pre. My middle name Du Pre, came from his name. His French sounding name actually came from Jersey where he was born in 1868. He was 74 when I was born and spoke fluent French.

He had been a friend of my Dad's family in Kent, for this was where my Dad moved from to become a trainee chef at the Midland Hotel in Manchester.

Uncle Jack had been a butler in the hotel and may have been the reason my Dad moved North with his family connections.

After his wife died, his family asked Dad to look after him as they were all still in Kent. That is how he came to live with us. In 1940, at the age of 74 he was a widower, I do not know why, but he was always my Uncle to me.

Editor's Note.

> *John Du Pré was born on 24 April 1868 in St. Lawrence, Jersey, his father, Tom, was 42 and his mother, Jane, was 32. He married Jane Elizabeth Laurens on 29 March 1891 in St. Helier, Jersey. They had one child during their marriage. He died in 1960 in Barton, Lancashire, at the age of 92. How he came to be in Manchester in 1940 is not known.*

Before the WW1 he was a carpenter in Jersey and in my days with him he taught me a lot of practical things.

I went to school in 1945 at the age of 5. My elementary school was called St. Brides on Moss Lane, ten minutes' walk away. Still walking on the toes of my left foot, you can imagine I was an easy target for the name calling of children and an easy target for bullying.

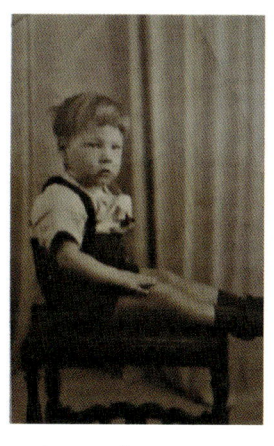

I was pushed over a lot. I would

come home covered in cuts and bruises. Never got any sympathy just a good telling off.

When I hurt myself, I just had to laugh it off. My Mum complained to the school but nothing was done. It was just kids playing!

I was not happy in these early years at school and Mum tried to get my leg treated but she was told that this could not be done until I was nine years old.

I didn't attend school regularly as a result and would take myself, off into the local park, Alexandra Park, where I would sit and watch the ducks. I would steal some bread from home to feed them.

I did a lot of thinking and talking to myself or the ducks if they were listening. Not that they could help me in any way. I was depressed, even at this young age, wondering what my life would be. I even thought of ending it all still so young.

But I thought, I am not going that way. I am going to work and get as much money as I can. When I did that it altered the conclusions for me, for that was the way I learned. The university of life experience.

I did not have much of an education but I could work. I used to run errands for people and do anything to earn money.

At the back of the house, an alley ran between the terraced houses. A few houses down the alley, lived a couple of elderly ladies who were bedridden. They would wait each day for a carer to come and get them out of bed. As they could not leave the house, they couldn't do their shopping for themselves.

In those days, doors were never locked. This allowed me to knock and enter without them getting out of bed. I would ask them for their shopping list and they would tell me which shops to go to. As I couldn't read, I had to hand these lists to the shopkeepers to make up the orders.

They would tell me to take the money out of their purse on the sideboard but I never did that, I was honest. I would give them the purse so that they could find the money and I always returned the change.

They wanted to pay me but I never took anything from them because they were disabled. I took money for other jobs however and I would buy saving stamps from the Post Office and put them in my little red books so that I did not spend what I had earned. In the end I had a whole stack of little red books and I knew exactly how many I had.

One day some were missing and I asked my Mum had she seen them. She told me she had been short of money. She had taken them to the Post Office and had cashed some.

I told her

"If you want money, ask me and I will give it to you but don't just take it."

She never did it again and I have to say over the years I helped my Mum out when she was short of money, because that is what you did. I worked very hard for it and when I wanted something for myself, I had the money with which I could buy it.

My Mum and Dad didn't have a lot of money, but my Dad worked very hard to keep us with his job and the two allotments he had. He grew vegetables and flowers, which were his pride and joy.

You can imagine that my limited life, my disability and lack of friends as I wasn't going to school, built on my attitude to life.

The school couldn't give me the care that I needed. I was frustrated and angry, not just with the world but with myself too. I was very short tempered and this didn't help my relationship with my Dad, as I would tell him what I thought; not a good idea in retrospect. We would argue all the time, a trend that continued through my teenage years

I wanted to talk to someone about my problems and the way I felt, but I had no one. My family were always too busy. My Mum couldn't help me. My Dad was always working and, on the two allotments he had. In that way, he would provide food and we

never wanted for anything. He was a good Dad in that way.

The age of nine arrived and I was now in a position to have treatment on my leg. I was admitted to Pendlebury Children's hospital in 1950 to have an operation to straighten my leg so that I could get my foot flat on the floor.

The surgeon, a small round man did the operation and I was in bed for eight weeks with my leg suspended in the air.

I don't know what he did but when the plaster came off my leg and they tried to get to me to learn to walk again, the operation wound burst open. I walked, fell over. Got up and fell again. Each time the wound split even more. So, he had to do it again.

Same procedure, leg in plaster, leg in the air, me in bed for eight weeks. Taking the plaster off for the second time, the wound failed once more.

This day however he was accompanied by a very tall man, a South African surgeon. You can imagine what they looked like, little and large. I thought it was funny.

The South African guy asked my first surgeon if he would mind if he did the third surgery. He was given the chance, "if you think you can do better than me".

I was off again for my third operation. This time when I woke up from the anaesthetic, I had a very sore backside. The surgeon had taken skin for my bum and used it to graft over the wound site.

Same procedure, leg in plaster, leg in the air, me in bed for eight weeks. When the plaster was removed this time, the wound had healed and didn't break open again.

All I had to do now was learn to walk. I would be in hospital for two years coming out shortly after my eleventh birthday and just before I was due to go to secondary school.

Editor's note.

> *It is likely that the problem that Jim had with his leg was down to a very short Achilles tendon which dragged the foot into a vertical position. The operation would have been to lengthen this. The failure of the first two attempts could well have been trying to stretch the limited amount of skin over the extended area. Too tight and it would burst open. The grafts cured this.*

I didn't want to come home. I wanted to stay in hospital. I felt safe there and everybody cared for me. I was a very popular patient.

The reason, I believe, was because I got the attention I craved for at home and didn't get. In hospital, I got on very well with the nurses and the other patients as I had a sense of humour which they appreciated.

Pendlebury hospital is in North Manchester and on the opposite side of the city to where my Parents lived. I don't know whether it was difficult for them to come and see me, but they would only come on occasionally on Saturdays. At least me Dad came, every Saturday. It was difficult for Mum to come as she couldn't travel on her own, not being able to read or write.

When my sisters were born, they got a lot of attention from my Dad. I don't think he liked boys he preferred to have daughters.

Before I went into hospital, I would spend time listening to the wireless (radio) as I wasn't going to school.

I remember listening to the broadcasts on Armistice day and each time, for two or three years I would cry at the thought of the soldiers who hadn't made it home.

After my oldest sister was born, we had to share the only bedroom as my Uncle had one and Mum and Dad the other. This sharing continued when my brother Peter joined us in 1950 and my sister Patricia in 1954.

Little privacy was had, and we had no bathroom.

Children in Shared Bedroom in Moss Side Moss Side, like we had to do

The tin bath would be brought in for bath night. Boys one night, girls the next. Hot water was produced from kettles boiling on the open coal fired range. When Mum and Dad bathed, I don't know.

The range had an oven alongside the open fire and Dad would put bricks in there to heat up. When hot, he would wrap them in towels to provide "hot water bottles" for the bedrooms.

When I came back from the hospital, life was alright for a time, but the arguments with my Dad started again. I did everything I could to please him.

I would help him make Christmas decorations at Christmas time from crepe paper, cut and made into chains. I would walk all over Manchester, knocking on doors and selling these. I never got any of that money and it was my idea to sell them in the first place.

I got the idea from a hairdresser shop across the road from the house, on Moss Lane East.

I noticed that each year they decorated their window for Christmas. I went in there one day and asked them if they would like to buy some decorations for the shop. They agreed and that was my first sale.

Shops on Moss Lane East

I would run errands for my Dad; fetch horse manure for his allotments and generally help. Never a thank you or a well done.

Chapter Two

Teenage Years

1952-1959

As you can imagine all those years of missed school and the two years in hospital without any education, my life was going to be difficult.

On attending secondary school, I still couldn't read or write and as a consequence I was considered backward. A term used in those days. I was put in a class for dunces.

This didn't go down very well with me because I knew I wasn't stupid, despite my Dad calling me that, throughout my childhood. My intelligence would surprise me throughout my life.

The school agreed to test me and I was sent for the test to a school in Chester. My Uncle took me to this massive school; I went everywhere with my Uncle as he was retired and my Dad was working and Mum couldn't read or write.

When I entered the class, I thought I was in the wrong place for the pupils there were what we called

Mongols in those days, more politely called children with Down's syndrome now. There were other mentally handicapped there too.

I was taken into a classroom on my own and asked to do simple tasks. Put bricks in the right shaped holes and things like that. This was very degrading to me and with my short temper I shouted at the teacher

"I'm not stupid. Why am I here? I have got more brains than this!"

You can imagine this didn't go down very well. The teacher spoke to my Uncle and I was thrown out. I had to go back to my dunces' class. This was not for me.

My Uncle was very good to me and he took me on my first holiday to Blackpool. We spent a week there staying in a small hotel where we had bed, breakfast and evening meal. I remember it very well because of a mishap I was responsible for.

We had eaten our breakfast and I said to him

"I am going out for a walk I will be back soon."

When I came back there were a lot of people milling around some thing had happened. The owner of the building told me that some one had left a tap running in a bathroom, with the plug in place. There was a flood.

I asked which room it was and it was our room. She thought my Uncle was responsible but I had to confess that was my fault.

She didn't tell me off, but thanked me for my honesty. I said

"I am always honest!"

This would be true for the rest of my life but did not always get me where I wanted to be.

As a consequence of the test failure in Chester and the return to school, I never attended very often, and never learned to read or write. The education authorities wrote to my Dad and told him I was not to go back because of my temper at the school. You can imagine what my Dad's reaction was.

I didn't go anywhere for a while, I kept getting odd jobs to get money for myself, but when I was thirteen a woman from social services told my Mum, she had found somewhere for me to go. It was a special school in Stretford, near the railway station.

When I went there, there were children with Downs syndrome and mentally and physically handicapped. I still didn't associate with them. It was not for me.

At break time, I crossed the school field and climbed over the fence to the station. I was running away and got a train home to Whalley Road station, just one stop down the line. When I got home, Mum said

Stool I made with woven seat

"What are you doing here?"

I said

"Mum, I don't know why I was put there in that school. They are all nutters."

She made me go back and eventually I got transport from an ambulance group. I became friendly with teachers, even they couldn't understand why I was there. They told my parents I was too intelligent to be there. I did learn handicrafts though which I have used throughout my life.

These problems of course created words with my Dad. I told him I am not backward but he continued to call me stupid over the years even then.

My Dad on his return from WW11 had taken a job with Manchester Corporation as a Park Keeper in Alexandra Park. Looking after the green houses and attending to the flower beds. He worked very hard and always managed to put food on the table. He was a good Dad in that way and I loved him for that, but I never got any love back. We always had a good family Christmas.

In the years when I was thirteen and fourteen the arguments with my Dad continued. My sister Sylvia was now seven, she was always very popular with my Dad, and my brother Peter was two. When I was fourteen my baby sister Patricia was born. The family was now four strong, all of them getting attention except me.

I had left school at fourteen in any case and I had been doing odd jobs. As I wasn't going to school, I would walk all over Manchester to amuse myself, bad leg or no bad leg. All alone. Following one big argument with my Dad he told me to leave the house and not come back.

I left and spent my nights sleeping rough. On park benches, in shop door ways. Life was hard. For money I would seek odd jobs here and there and following my early childhood decisions to work if nothing else, that brought me through.

I remember clearly one job I did. It had snowed heavily and the pavements were deep in snow blocking shop entrances on Moss Lane. I tried the first shop and asked if they would like the snow cleared. Asked how much it would cost, I said

"half a crown" (two shillings and sixpence).

They agreed and I manged to get all the shops lined up. Back home to fetch a shovel and broom, I returned and cleared the whole stretch of Moss Lane East. Content, tired and a pocket full of money. A good day's work done.

Sleeping on the Park benches was risky, for my Dad worked in that Park so I had to be up and about before he came to work. Fortunately, it was summer time and I didn't get cold.

After a few months, my Uncle found me and persuaded me to come back home, which I did and it was alright for a while. However, when I was fifteen, my Dad said

"You are fifteen now. You need to take some responsibility for the family. If you want to stay here you need to get a job!"

What could I do, I needed a job? I found this job working in the kitchen canteen at Thomas French's a company that made curtains.

They were situated at Chester Road Mills, Manchester, 15. And had a London office at Oxford Street, W1. (1947)

I was employed as a pot boy, clearing all the dirty plates and doing the washing up. I worked with the chef there, a Jewish lady who was very kind to me and I became fascinated watching her working. One night after I had finished my work, she was preparing pastry for the following days meals and I asked could I watch her. She said

"I can teach you how to do this if you like?"

I was pleased to have the offer. She wrote a letter and asked me to give it to my Dad when I got home. I didn't know what was in the letter, I couldn't have read it in any case. Giving it to my Dad when he came home from work, he said

"What's this?"

I told him the story of the offer from the Jewish lady. After he read the letter he said,

"Don't be stupid. You can't do that. You're stupid!"

That was not a nice thing to say, but I was not surprised. I was never appreciated over the years. Many times, I asked him

"Why do you call me stupid?" I

never got an answer.

"Am I disappointment to you. I have helped you a lot in my life but you have never given me praise." Still no answer.

The following morning, he gave me a letter to give back to the Jewish chef. Again, I did not know what it said but when she read it, it must have been a very rude letter because it upset her. She apologised for getting me into trouble. She didn't have to do that as it wasn't her fault.

I only stayed in the job for about a year for I couldn't stand the heat in the kitchen. I am a very hotblooded person and the heat got to me. When I told her I was leaving, she thought it was because of the trouble she had caused but I told it was not her fault.

Editor's Note.

Thomas French.

1950 Just as gun belts had led to the original development of Rufflette tapes, so the engineering skills developed in progressing from woven gun belts to metal articulated belts lead to more improvements in the firm's product range. Increasingly sophisticated curtain fittings, and an amazingly diverse range of products were now being made.

At home, public pressure for Do It Yourself products pushed sales of Rufflette products to an all-time high. Consumers showed that they wanted brand names they knew and when a leading UK store introduced its own ready-made curtains for the first time, they were to advertise them as having Rufflette tape headings.

Rufflette was one of the first products to be advertised on the new ITV channel.

When I was sixteen, I got a job working with Greyhounds at Belle Vue Greyhound Stadium.

Chapter Three
The Belle Vue Years
1956 - 1958

I got the job working with the Greyhounds from a speculative turn up at the main office at Bellevue when I was sixteen.

I went to the main office and asked if there were any jobs available. Luckily for me the man in the office was the manager of the Greyhound Stadium. He was also a trainer of Greyhounds for he owned twelve of his own.

He wanted me to join the team of kennel boys and girls who looked after all the dogs that lived in the kennels at the back of the Greyhound stadium.

Jim outside the White City Greyhound track 1956

Belle Vue Zoological Gardens
were originally meant to be an enjoyable pastime for the middle classes, however they very quickly became one of the North West's biggest attractions. At the height of Belle Vue's popularity it was host to around 2 million visitors a year. The site eventually became home to exotic animals, live music, dancing, speedway, boxing and wrestling, greyhound racing, football, rugby league and a myriad of other entertainments.

Just about anyone who spent time in Manchester, prior to Belle Vue finally closing its doors in 1987, has a story to tell about it.

I liked animals, despite the dog bites from the Yorkshire terrier who dragged out of my pram along the back entry all those years ago, when I could have lost my arm. My Mum had been told this by the people at the hospital.

She also told me later that after a police enquiry, the Yorkshire Terrier was found and put down, for it had a history of biting people.

At the Greyhound stadium. I worked for a trainer called Percy. He was the general manager of the Greyhound Track at Belle Vue but he had his own dogs. There were twelve that belonged to him and they lived in the kennels at the back of the stadium.

We would feed them, clean them out and walk them when they were not in training. I worked well with the kennel maids and lads, and got on generally well with all the people, for I was always polite.

When there were race meetings on, the first thing we had to do was take the dogs who were racing, to the Vets, to make sure they were fit to run. If they were passed fit, we would parade them in front of the grandstand and put them in their traps ready for the race. I had to wear a Bowler hat and a White coat. I did look a character in that hat!

I travelled with the Greyhounds to meetings at the White City in Manchester. To tracks in Birmingham and London. We did this on a special bus with kennels in the back.

I can't remember any of the Dogs names. None of them became champions but we did have some winners. When that happened, we quite often got backhanders from owner.

There were Bitches and Dogs and we had to be careful to keep them apart. When out walking, to exercise them, we tried to keep a distance apart from each group, as we would have several dogs in hand.

One day, a lad with his group got too close to a maid who had a group of bitches, his were dogs. The bitches were on heat and he could not stop the stampede towards them.

In his attempt to separate the brawl, he got in amongst the fighting animals and received dog bites. He was hospitalised with over one hundred and fifty bites. He never came back to the job.

I had my favourite dogs, but if any one of them got an injury, they were no longer useful to the trainers. Some became pets; however, the majority were put to sleep there and then by the Vets.

I didn't like this action, nor did I like the way the bodies were disposed of, for we had to take them in a wheelbarrow to the main Boiler house, where they were thrown on the fire.

Not a nice part of my job and this was the reason I left after two years.

When I had been fifteen, I had the first pint of beer of my life. I had an errand to run each week for my Dad, taking money to pay his Union fees. These were collected in the upstairs room of a local pub. One night my Dad said

"While you are there, get yourself a pint."

After paying the fees I went into the bar and asked for a pint of mild. The barman looked at me a little suspiciously but I got my pint nevertheless.

Problems were always part of my life. One day I came home from work at the Greyhound track, and the young woman who lived upstairs, the Polish men had left, was with my Mum crying. There were bricks in our living room which had fallen down the chimney. I said

"What has happened here?"

They both said that they didn't know but the young woman couldn't get into her room, the door wouldn't open and her baby son was in there in his cot.

I went upstairs to try and help. But the door was stuck. I got an axe and broke down one of the panels in the door so that I could crawl through. I cut my head on the broken door in my haste to do it.

What I found was a big shock. The roof had fallen in. There were bricks and slates everywhere and it was these that were blocking the door.

I could just see the cot under all the rubble, but there were bricks in there too. I climbed over everything and removed as much as I could from the cot and found the little boy. Fortunately, he was not injured badly just a few cuts and bruises.

We called an ambulance, it was the St, John's ambulance in those days and he was taken to the hospital to be checked over. I think I saved his life that day.

The house was declared unsafe and we had to move. Where the woman with the baby went, I don't know. We couldn't stay there and we went to live with a friend of my Dad's temporarily. All six of us lived in one room.

He lived in a house further down Sloane Street. The move was in November 1955. We stayed there till after Christmas in one room. There were many people in that house, apart from us. There was my Dad's friend, his wife, a Mate and his Mum.

It was so crowded that we left our furniture in the derelict house. We were not supposed to go back there but when we did find a house we had to enter and retrieve our belongings.

My Dad applied to the council for a house, but at first, they wanted to split the family up, putting us children in a home. My Mum said it was a workhouse and she wasn't going to have that and stood her ground.

A few weeks into the New Year, we were given a house in Addison Crescent in Old Trafford, in a cul-de-sac at first, but we weren't there long because my Dad wanted a bigger garden. We moved to Lime Crescent just across the main Addison Crescent Road.

My Uncle couldn't come with us and he went to live in an old folks' home on the Talbot Road in Stretford, close to the Lancashire cricket ground.

This was because my Dad had objected to him coming. In 1960 he fell out of bed in the home, injured his head on the radiator when he fell, and eventually died in Davyhulme hospital in a few months later.

For the fifteen years he had been with us he had been very close to me and helped me a lot along the way. I missed his company.

After leaving the Greyhound track, I tried many jobs to get work. I worked in an Engineering firm in Old Trafford, but my foreman was not a nice man. We had a fight which came to blows, me being stubborn and him being arrogant.

He reported me to the boss who had me in his office for an explanation. The foreman had been there before me. The boss took his side and I walked before I was sacked. I had been there three weeks.

I moved on to work in a soap factory but only lasted there for two weeks. My third job in the years 17 to 19 years of age was in a factory belonging to Regent Rubber.

My job was in the depths of the factory with very little lighting. It was very dark down there. I had to stand by a big barrel of French talk and as the sheets of rubber came along a huge conveyer belt, I had to throw fistfuls of chalk onto the rubber. This was so the sheets did not stick together when piled up.

I had been there three days when in the darkness, someone placed a wheelbarrow behind the barrel of chalk and left the handles sticking out.

Walking backwards I fell over the handles and in saving myself, landed on my right hand and broke a bone. I was taken to the hospital and put in plaster.

The following day I was back to see the boss who wanted a report. When he saw my hand in plaster, he said

"You are no use to us with that," pointing to my plaster cast. He sacked me there and then. No health and safety rules in those days.

When my hand was healed, I got a job working in the building trade with a man who had a business in Union Street off the Stretford Road. It was based in what used to be the stables for police horses and the place from where I got my Dad's manure for his allotments.

I was a joiner, for my Uncle had been a carpenter and he had taught basic skills. I worked there till I was twenty-one, but as that birthday approached, the boss said to me

"I can't afford to pay you a man's wage after your birthday so I will have to let you go!"

I would have been entitled to a wage rise at twenty-one having reached the age of maturity, but then again, I had no job.

My ever-seeking job search managed to find me work for King Pin Flour Mill which was situated in central Manchester off Upper Brook Street. I was employed in the department responsible for the cleaning of the flour sacks.

These cloth sacks had been returned, used and we had to place them under a huge vacuum machine which sucked all the dirt and flour remains out of them so that they could be used again.

I used to work at weekends too. When I was at Bell Vue, I worked for a very rich man who had a big house in the countryside and I would look after his garden. He had Greyhounds at the track.

He asked me to work at weekends away from the track and he would collect me from the stadium, take me to his house and I would stay the night when there were no race meetings. On the Sunday he would bring me back to Belle Vue for me to catch a bus home.

He was very good to me and I did a good job for him. He was very pleased with the work I did and he would pay me thirty pounds for a weekends work. I did this for a few years but gave it up when I got married at twenty-one.

Chapter Four

Life with My Dad

1940 – 1959

James Richard Deal was born on 19 May 1913 in Molash, Kent, his father, Samuel, was 31 and his mother, Sarah, was 32. He married Mary Roberts on 20 May 1939. They had four children in 14 years. He died on 1 January 2002 in Manchester, Lancashire, at the age of 88, and his death was registered in Barton, Cheshire.

As you can see from the school picture below, my Dad was from a large family in Kent. I don't know when he came to Manchester but the reason, he was in Manchester originally, was to become a chef in the Midland hotel on Peter Street.

In 1939, he married my Mum and I was born in 1940.

My life with him became difficult on the day I was born.

I know my Mum had three children before I was born, who had died in early infancy or had been still born, and whether this had coloured my Dad's view of me when I was born, I don't know.

In his eyes he had a son who wasn't perfect and after the three disappointments before he felt let down yet again, as I was born with a deformed leg and two ruptures. At three pound eight ounces I was not supposed to live long, but I did.

In the first three years of my life I was nothing but a trouble to him, with all the hospital visits, failure to sit up when I should have been and even then, began walking on my left toes.

My failure to mix with other kids, falls, scrapes and bruises, all had to be dealt with.

By the age of five and the prospect of school, more problems came from the inability of the school to give me not only education but care. Not able to stop the bullying, being pushed over, coming home with injuries. All problems for the family. But never sympathy from my Dad.

My increasing frustration with life, my short temper as a result, caused the arguments we had.

Unfortunately for me, I was a determined individual even when young and I would not let him win when I knew he was wrong.

Many a clip round the ear, and yet I loved him and I wanted him to love me back. He never gave me any indication of that. I always loved everybody in my family.

Between the age of five and nine, my inability to go to school left me wondering what my life would be like. I had no friends so had to entertain myself.

Mum and Dad were always busy and I had no help from them as regard my worries.

My state of mind, depressed had pushed me close to thinking about ending my life but I talked myself out of that with the aid of the ducks.

I had a three-way choice. To the right I would end up with gangs and crime. To the left suicide and straight through the middle a life of hard work, continuing bad leg or no bad leg.

My Dad did not seem to notice my problems. He never asked me how I was and he was never there for me to tell him. I tried to please him in the only way I could and that was to do as much work for him, in whatever way he wanted me too.

I remember clearly, that as we didn't have a lot of money, Dad would make our Christmas decorations. He would buy different coloured rolls of crepe paper and cut them so that each circle could be made part of a multi-coloured chain. He had a workshop in the basement, where he would make toys too.

Lead model soldiers and cowboys from scrap lead he had found or "acquired" was heated on his primus stove and poured in to moulds he had. Each figure, be they soldiers, Cowboys or Indians he hand painted. He made forts for the soldiers from orange boxes that I would collect for him from the greengrocers.

He would put towers in each of the corners and a draw bridge which would go up and down and applied plaster to the outside, roughly, making it look like stone by painting it grey.

Across the road from our house was a lady's hairdressers who would add decorations at Christmas to their window. I went there and asked them if they would like me to bring some for them. They agreed and I went and told my Dad who gave me some decorations to take over the road.

I asked fourpence (d) for them and they paid without question. Many of the customers wanted them too; I fetched some more from my Dad and sold all those.

This gave me an idea that others would buy, so I walked miles, bad leg or no bad leg, knocking on doors and selling my wares.

I was out many nights before Christmas each year selling the decorations and wouldn't come home until all were sold. I had made a special box to carry them in and that had to be empty before I came home. This was an egg box with string attached to go around my head.

Pendlebury Children's Hospital. I am second on left

All the money in my bulging pockets that I had collected, I gave to my Dad and got not a penny in return. Not even a thank you or well-done son. This didn't stop me trying to please him.

At nine, in hospital for my operations, my Dad never came to see me. I got a lot of attention from the nurses and Doctors and with my sense of humour entertained the other patients.

This attention was new to me and I liked and I didn't want to come home, but I had to. Dad and me got on quite well for a while until the schooling problems began to cause trouble.

I continued to do jobs for him in my early teenage years. I would push an old pram for miles to collect the horse manure for his allotments. I don't know where the pram came from, but it must have been used for me, Sylvia and Peter, for she was now seven and he was four.

The pram was similar to the one in the picture but I would put the hood up and build up the sides with planks of wood so that it would carry more load.

God it was heavy when full and the smell was unbelievable.

> At home I would keep out of his way as much as possible and I entertained myself by going to the cinema, on my own, a different one each time as there were several close by that I could walk to.

I paid for this with the money I earned doing odd jobs. One I clearly remember was the Claremont in Moss Side.

As I have said before, when I was fifteen my Dad said

"If you want to continue living here, you had better get a job. As the eldest you have a responsibility to help support the Family," and "when you get that first wage packet don't you dare open it."

I did get that first job in the kitchen at Thomas French and I got my first wage packet.

Dutifully I brought it home and gave it to my Dad who opened and gave me five bob, (shillings), keeping the rest himself. I don't know to this day how much it was.

This was to be the pattern for all my wages going forward and from that five bob I had to clothe myself and by my own shoes. On one occasion I came out of work on a Wednesday, unusually they paid on a Wednesday, and it was pouring with rain.

I had no money in my pockets but I thought I don't want to get wet, I will open my wage and use that to take a bus home instead of walking.

When I got home, I handed over my wage packet. My Dad said

"You have opened this. I told you not do that!" With a clip round the ear, he didn't want to hear why I had done that even though it was still pouring outside.

I left school at fourteen and he threw me out. He thought I would come back but I didn't. I slept rough on Park benches or anywhere I could. Nobody knew where I was and it wasn't the only time that I would be thrown out.

I did go back after a short time because my Uncle wanted me to go back to him. We tried to make a go of it, and he did alright for a while but it all started again.

Another Birthday came around and I was another year older. I carried on but we were always arguing;

I was always in trouble. In an argument I was saying this is me. Why can't you accept that!

I helped my Mum: I was very good to her because she was very like me, she couldn't move me in my attitude to Dad, but she was a good Mum. Dad was a good Dad too, but I never understood why we didn't get on. I loved my Dad but it didn't work out.

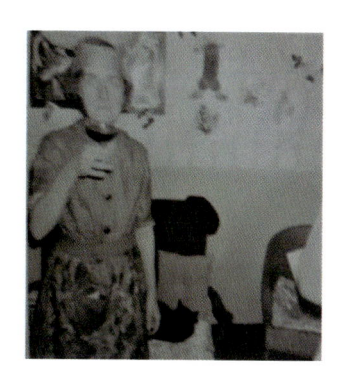

He threw me out again, but I didn't go back that time. I found a very small flat with no furniture. It was a single room in a house on Seymour Grove. I had knocked on their door to ask for help and the lady who answered said she had a spare room I could use.

I slept on the floor, sleeping rough for a few weeks but at least I was dry. I got a few jobs and got some money together to buy a few things

I went to Blackpool and slept rough there for a while but as it was summertime it was much better. I did a few jobs to earn as much money as I could, where ever I could.

People use to say to me

"The trouble with you and your Dad is because you are like two peas in a pod. Neither of you will give in."

I said

"It is not the same. You don't know my Dad as well as you think you do; not like I do. If I am right, I will stick to my guns and nobody will change it."

That was the way it was and many years later I got out from under his moods.

I went to several places, I could get on with people easily, this allowed me to earn money when I could.

Living in that one room flat, I always went back home when my Dad was working and I would give my Mum some money to help her out. She smoked a lot and needed the money to buy cigarettes. I deliberately went at that time to avoid my Dad.

I did as many jobs outside of my usual work to get as much money as I could. I always worked hard; I soldiered on.

Eventually, he got over his moods and he wanted me to go back home. I said to myself

"I am not going back to anywhere where my Dad is!"

My Mum wanted me to come back.

I did go back to see my Dad, not that I wanted to but unfortunately, in 1958, Dad got ill and went into hospital. It had been difficult for him and going to work in the winter time was worse.

He was very poorly. Everybody at the hospital did what they could for him, but he was in hospital a very long time and ended up in a special hospital in Eccles. He had a problem with his lung.

For long while he couldn't work when he was home again, as he was too weak. The family came all together and we did what we could to help out financially.

The hospital in Eccles was not far from when I used to go and see Pearl in Irlam, I would make an effort to see him too. They were very good to him but it left him very weak. We all had to do as much as we could and pay for the regular shopping.

We all had to be checked out to see if we had the same problem as my Dad because the problem could have spread to all of us.

Fortunately, we were all clear, which was a miracle really. I went back home to help my Mum and the family all pulled together like we always did.

When he didn't get well quickly, he started moaning again. For a long time, I wished I wasn't staying there for I had my own troubles with Pearl. I didn't tell him that, I lied for a while.

Eventually he did go back to work but he was more fussy after that. He would often take a side but I was being wise for the future, keeping my thoughts to myself.

However, many times, he was wrong and I knew he was wrong and would tell him he was wrong; he didn't like it. As you can imagine, we fell out again. This time I didn't give a monkeys! I was working.

All was well with Dad for a few years and I had got the job as the joiner. Inevitably we fell out again. I was a very determined individual and I would stand up to him.

This time I found myself a little flat. I had no furniture and I had to sleep on the floor but at least it was my own flat. Of course, when I was twenty-one and lost my job, I couldn't afford the rent so I had to go back home.

My relationship with my Dad didn't improve when I got married.

Editor's Note

> *The fact that Jim mentions a special hospital for his Dad with a lung problem and that the family were all clear, would indicate that his Dad had tuberculosis. This was quite prevalent in the slum conditions of Manchester at that time.*

Chapter Five
My First Marriage
1962 - 1963

I first met Pearl, who would become my first wife, when I was sixteen. I had been going to a club for disabled people, held in the evenings in a school hall in Stretford. Friends had told me about it.

We would play cards. Be entertained by singers and dancers and have trips out into the countryside. We visited historic buildings and mansions and even had a trip to Southport to see the sea. Not that it is always visible there because it goes out for miles.

I made good friends there. One girl, also disabled, who I knew and lived just around the corner from me in Lime Crescent, had a friend called Pearl who lived in Irlam, North West Manchester. This particular weekend, she had invited this Pearl, who too was disabled, to come and stay with her for the weekend. She was eighteen.

She asked me to go around and meet Pearl when she was there. I think I fell in love with her at first sight, her eyes were so beautiful. Pearl was only small, about four feet tall. She had jet-black hair and brown eyes. I fell in love with those eyes.

She had had a difficult childhood because her mother, who was only 29, died in childbirth,; her Father was the same age. She was born in West Derby Liverpool.

At birth she was born with a deformed hip and spent her early years in hospital, Biddulph Grange

Orthopaedic, for treatment to correct this. She would walk with the aid a stick all her life.

Her Dad couldn't look after as he was working so she was brought up by an Aunty in Irlam until she was sixteen, when she went back to live with her Dad. She was living there when I first met her. She was two years older than me.

Biddulph Grange Orthopaedic Hospital Patients outside in the summer

Editor's note

> In 1922 Biddulph Grange was sold to the North Staffordshire Cripples Aid Society to use as a hospital. Within 3 years the Society could no longer afford it so it went to Lancashire County Council as a hospital.

They built wooden wards on the cherry orchard and later in the 1930s, knocked down the remaining glass houses and part of the geological gallery to build new wards and a 'modern' hospital complex during which time the house was used as nurses' quarters.

The house served as a children's hospital from 1923 until the 1960s; known first as the "North Staffordshire Cripples' Hospital" and later as the "Biddulph Grange Orthopaedic Hospital" (though it took patients with non-orthopaedic conditions as well. Under this latter title the hospital's role expanded to accommodate adults, continuing in operation into the mid-1980s.

Following our first meeting at her friend's house, I was invited to Irlam to meet her Dad for she had no Mum.

Pearl told me he was a very nice man when he was sober, but could be quite violent when drunk. He was a steel worker in the Steel works in Eccles, Manchester.

Pearl told me she would lock herself in her bedroom when he came home drunk and hide for safety. He did this most days on payday, having spent time in the pub on the way home, new wages in his pocket.

Pearl never worked with her disability and she was highly strung. We had similar characteristics. After my first visit I used to cycle all the way to Irlam and we went to a disabled club in nearby Urmston, as well as the one in Stretford. I would cycle home to Lime crescent, Old Trafford.

Pearl was not a well person and she was always in and out of hospital. In 1959 she was taken ill and put in a hospital in Oswestry in Shropshire. This was a specialist orthopaedic hospital; she was to be there a very long time. She had lost the use of her legs and couldn't walk.

She had always had a limp and used a stick to help her balance, but even then, she would walk badly; the Doctors and nurses were trying to get her to walk again. She was twenty-two years old and would receive a lot of physiotherapy treatment but was always in pain. They could only give her pain relief medication.

When she first got ill and couldn't walk, she was very frightened, not helped when she was admitted to the hospital in Oswestry. It was a wonderful hospital but quite far from home. She was there a very long time but that gave me a bit more time to save more money.

Not that I wanted her to be there all that time. I was saving money because I wanted to go and see her every week. I would go up on a Sunday and more than once stay in the lodgings across the road from the hospital. Stay overnight and come back on Sunday ready for work the next day.

Times were hard but I did it. I am a very determined person. I did what I could. It was very, very difficult but I did it. I was very proud of myself I have to say.

Editor's Note.

It is likely that Pearl not only suffered a deformed hip at birth but had a severe scoliosis which made her lean to the left, exaggerating the hip problem. It was suspected but never proven that her mother, whilst pregnant had taken a beating from her drunken, violent husband, may be another reason why Pearl locked herself away when he was in that state,

Oswestry is a long way from Manchester and the first time I visited her I took the train. It was a long journey. I stayed with her for a couple of hours and took the train home. I used to visit on a Sunday, as I was working on the Saturday. Occasionally, I would go down on the Saturday and stay the weekend.

After that first visit, I discovered that there was a bus that went there and I could catch it in Piccadilly Gardens bus station in Central Manchester. The bus took its time and we would stop for a meal on the way. Not getting back to Manchester until after seven in the evenings. It cost one pound and ten shillings.

I wanted to be with longer than a few hours, but I didn't know where to stay. When I knocked on a door of a house across the road from the hospital to ask if they knew anywhere.

The lady who answered the door said I could stay there and that is what I did. No one else visited Pearl while she was in hospital there.

She was always waiting for me when I walked in, sitting up in bed smiling. After she had been there a month the nurses would get her out of bed and put her in a chair for my visits. We used chat and have a laugh and she was very well liked by all the hospital staff and for some reason I was too.

She came out after Christmas in 1960 and was alright for many months. We enjoyed the summer with our trips, but the winter of 1960/1961 was a bad one, heavy snow and she got ill again. This time she was taken back to Oswestry to recover.

My visits continued throughout the spring and she was home again in the summer of 1961. This wasn't to last however, for the winter of 1961/1962 was even worse and she got pneumonia, but this time she recovered, and we had the summer together.

During her time in Oswestry we had talked about getting married but of course that was going to be expensive and our savings were small. We did plan however and Pearl would talk to the nurses and doctors about it.

On one visit in early 1962, Pearl told me that the Doctor wanted talk to me and could I come the following weekend on a Saturday to see him. Which I did.

I was worried because I knew she had a mouth on her, and wondered whether she had said something to upset them. But she said you have nothing to worry about.

The Doctor took me into his office where we could talk. Me having nothing to worry about apologised but as I wasn't there if she had upset them. He did talk about that, but the real reason was not that, he said

"I believe you are talking about getting married."

I said

"Yes, but we can't afford to do that at the moment we haven't got enough money." He said

"Have you thought about getting married here in Oswestry?

I replied

"It would be nice but I can't afford to do that, it would be even more expensive." He answered me straight away

"It won't cost you anything. It will be all arranged, the vicar, the registrar and a reception. I am not at liberty to tell you who will pay for this but it will be free to you both."

I went back to the ward to tell Pearl who was quite excited. I asked her to hang on because the Doctor had asked me to give it a week to think about it and let him know next time I came.

I went home and got hold my Mum and Dad and told them. My Dad said

"Don't be stupid. I can't afford to go there so that you can get married and you are stupid marrying her in the first place. You are far too young". I was twenty-one and Pearl was twenty-three.

My Dad never liked Pearl but my Mum did. He wasn't very helpful in that way. I said

"I can't worry about what you think! In any case, we are getting married very young whether you like it or not!"

"If I do get married, and if you want to come to the wedding you can do but if you don't want to, you don't have to."

I had never got on well with my Dad in any case. As much as I loved him, and I loved him very much, I knew what I was going to do. I had a mind of my own as I am a very determined person.

I went back to the Doctors in Oswestry and told them

"It won't work because my Dad won't come down to the wedding."

Two months went by and I had a very good side-line as well as my job, working for a very rich person. I told him

"I am saving very hard all the money I am earning so that my Mum and Dad can come to the wedding,"

I had saved hard for the wedding in any case, but when I told him about my Mum and Dad, he gave extra money.

I worked extra hours. I worked very hard. After I told him my Mum and Dad couldn't afford to come to the wedding, he gave a bit more. It was very good of him and he helped me a lot.

He asked me if I would go and do some work in his garden. He said he would pick me up and take me there and bring me back to catch the bus home. I did that every year Pearl was in hospital. He paid me very well and I was working in the countryside. So, I did alright.

Any time I had a chance to earn money, I was there like a shot. I was always willing to work and not frightened of getting my hands dirty. I was well known for that.

It was very hard and I was on my own most of the time. It was very hard to do these things and sometimes I didn't know what to do for the best.

I was still going to see Pearl. Eventually, I said to Pearl

"I am going to see your Doctor. Can you tell him I want to see him when I come down next weekend?"

I went to see the Doctor on the Saturday morning. He was a very nice person. I told him I had been thinking about what he had offered and I had worked my socks off to earn quite a bit of money. I told him

"I have to get my Dad to the Church and the wedding. I have to pay him to come, otherwise he wouldn't come down." I had told my Dad

"If you don't come, we are getting married anyway, and I won't let that stop me."

I am a very determined person once I have made my mind up. As it happens, I said to him

"Come down for the weekend and I will put you up in a guest house and I will pay for that! I will pay your bus fare and meals in the guest house as well." So, he and my Mum did come down. It was hard work for me because I had to find all the money. Money which was hard to get and for which I had worked and saved hard.

The doctor had said we could get married in Oswestry and they would make all the arrangements. They would do that because Pearl was liked and she talks about you. When you come here and talk to her, you get on very well with the nurses and they like you too.

We did very well didn't we! Everybody liked us.

I went back to Pearl and said

"When do you want to get married, because

everything is sorted."

We were married a few weekends later in August 1962, in a church on a hill in Oswestry, St Martins Parish Church. The arrangements had been made with the vicar and a reception was booked in the church hall where a buffet had been laid out.

The guest list was Mum and Dad, Pearls Dad and one of her Auntie's. My best man was a friend of Pearls, Rupert; his wife was there too. Rupert was a friend of Pearls who lived in Old Trafford; Pearls best friends' mate was his wife. My sister Sylvia was a bridesmaid.

Rupert had arranged to bring my Mum and Dad down by car, so that they didn't have to make arrangements to get there.

Pearl's wedding dress was made by a friend who owned a dress shop in Irlam. She looked very good and I was dead chuffed.

I had to get a suit. I went to Burtons but all the suits were too expensive. There was one on display, all big checks. I asked if they would do deal a deal on that one, which they did. I looked like a chess board. It had huge bell bottom trousers. Pearl liked it. I didn't and never wore it again after the wedding.

The doctor had told me that he was not at liberty to say who paid for it all. All I had to do was turn up and everything would be there.

Pearl was allowed out of hospital for a week after the wedding ceremony and we had a honeymoon in a Pub in Blackburn. Pearl new the landlord. She did however have to go back in hospital after that. It was the summer time of 1962.

When I took her back, I asked the doctor how long she was likely to be there. He said

"Unfortunately, she will be her for some time yet."

It was sad in one sense, but good in another because it would give me time to find suitable accommodation for when she does come out. It will also give me time to save some more money to do what we did do for it turned out very good.

It did take time to find a place and we had very little money, just enough to get a little flat, not far from my Parents, near to the Manchester United football ground in Old Trafford, Railway Road.

Railway. Road, present day

I

pg. 71

kept myself busy while she was still in the hospital, working on my garden at the back of the flat as well as working at King Pin.

The grass was about three feet high when I first got there. I cut it all down, dug over the patch and laid a proper lawn

In the middle, I cut out a circle and planted roses and the whole thing was surrounded by a fence which I made myself.

The neighbours in the flats above us were very appreciative of my work, for it gave a much better outlook than the drab railway line and signal box.

Workers outside King Pin, me on the right

There were couples there who didn't get on with their parents – we had a shared experience – they had troubles over a potential marriage. I would take them

aside and offer advice. I became very good at talking to them because I was very understanding. It did good because I achieved approval from both sides of the problem

Pearl and I did alright for a while with hospital visits, but unfortunately, things went pear shaped and she got very ill again and it was coming up to Christmas time 1962. My Mum was able to come and see her before Christmas day.

After Christmas she started to pick up and pleased the Doctors. I was able to bring her home. The doctors had been very good to her.

We did alright for a while for it was the summer of 1963 and I took her to Southport. The social workers had found a place where she could stay and be paid for, but I had to pay for myself. I was able to do that for I had money saved.

I had to make arrangements at work to stay for a fortnight. I didn't mind that for I didn't want to leave her alone. The encouraging thing was she got better and we had a nice time.

At Southport, more often than not the water is miles out to sea. We had as good a time as we could under the circumstances. Where we were staying, the people were wonderful but it had to come to an end. We came home to our flat so that I could go back to work.

The flat was in a three-storey block of flats on Railway Road, the end of a series of apartment blocks on that road. The view at the back was of the Manchester United football ground, obviously not as grand as it is now.

I had a good friend who lived upstairs who would pop in everyday to see how she was, when I was at work. He lived upstairs and worked shifts so was home most afternoons.

He had first come down in the middle of a thunderstorm. He was frightened even though he was around thirty years of age. I used to joke with Pearl that she had another man on the side. He spent some time with her which was nice of him.

I was working hard, as hard as I did on any job and I would pop home at dinner time to make some dinner for her and for when I got home in the evening. This way I could make sure she was alright.

Sometimes, I would come home earlier in the evenings and we would discuss what problems I had during the day. She was very good at that, a really good listener. She would tell me what was going on at home and what the neighbours were doing.

At work, I finished any time I could, but sometimes, there was a bit of overtime, which I didn't mind. I never said no to it, the extra money for a couple of hours work would be very nice.

Occasionally, I would start early to come home early and my boss was very happy with that; he never objected. He understood what problems I had and how much attention I wanted to give to Pearl now that she was home. He was wonderful, a lovely man, a best friend regardless of our position. We did very well by him.

I had a mate at work whose name was Jim as well. We had some laughs along the way. Pearl and I got one very well for some time, then things went pear-shaped again. She got pneumonia again in the November of 1963, another very bad winter and was admitted this time to Park Hospital in Davyhulme, Manchester. This was much easier for me to visit.

At the same time my Sister, Sylvia, was in the same hospital. My brother had told me. My Mum asked me to go and see her when I was visiting Pearl. I told her that Pearl was in a ward downstairs. Sylvia said

"I hope she is alright."

I said

"She is not. She has pneumonia and very poorly. I will keep you posted."

I asked how she was and Sylvia answered

"Not so bad. I have a problem."

I can't remember for the life of me what was wrong with Sylvia, but I did the job Mum asked me to do. She was very pleased to see me as neither Mum or Dad had been. They always said they were too busy. Sylvia understood and said

"Tell them not to worry."

When I got home, I told my Mum that I had seen Sylvia when I had gone to see Pearl. I told her that Pearl was doing okay and that I had explained to her that you were tied up and couldn't get there. Sylvia has said you are not worry about her.

As you can imagine it was a really bad, difficult time. I was so tired, working, going home, getting changed and going to the hospital to see Pearl.

I was trying to find out how she was doing. Was she in pain? Whatever? But it was all down to her. She was fighting very hard, fighting the illness. It was very hard for her and she was well aware of that.

I had a word with the Doctors, for she was very frightened and I was worried. They said

"She is very, very poorly. We are doing all we can, but in the end, it is down to her. She is fighting it but she is very weak and only time will tell."

Pearl started to recover and I was able to bring her home. I was glad to see her there and we did our best to help her recover.

The stay was very short lived as she went downhill again and was back in hospital. I sked the Doctor

"What are her chances?"

He replied

"There are medicines that work and sometimes it can turn around but it takes time to work. The problem is she has only the one lung. We will have to see over the next few days."

I used to chat to her as though we were talking. She couldn't reply because she had an oxygen mask over her face. Bless her. That was the way it was and eventually she would fall asleep, I would leave her in peace and go home.

By this time, Sylvia had got better and had gone home after being discharged from the hospital.

Yet again it was coming up to Christmas time. It was difficult for Pearl and me, more so for her because she was the one in hospital. For me it was difficult because we only had one day off, that was Christmas Day and we would be back at work on Boxing day.

A friend of mine took me down by car on Christmas Day and left me there coming back later to pick me up. He was very good to me in that way. We spent the day as best we could but she was very ill.

I went to work the next day, Boxing Day, and I hadn't been there very long when I got a message that the boss wanted to see me. I went up to his office and when I walked in there was a policeman there. When you see that you know there is something wrong, don't you?

The policeman told me that Pearl had died in the early hours of the morning and that I needed to go to the hospital to get things sorted. I went home first and cried as you can imagine.

I went to tell me Mum and Dad that Pearl had passed away and I was very upset there too. I stayed there with them that day and night. In the morning my Dad came down and we had a chat about what I had to do at the hospital. I needed to see the Doctors to find out what went wrong.

Unfortunately, there had to be an inquest and that wasn't possible over the Christmas period. I had to wait a few days before we could go to the hospital to find things out.

When we did go those few days later, I found out that she only had one lung and the pneumonia had been too much for her.

She had never told me that, if she knew herself. If she did know it was a bit naughty of her on her part really. That is why the pneumonia made it very difficult for her to breath, and why she struggled with the illnesses and became poorly so quickly.

She never told me, but I loved her and forgave her, but that is why I didn't know it could get so bad in such a short time. I didn't mind that she hadn't told me but I was so upset as you can imagine. At the end of the day I had to carry on and that is what I did.

EDITOR'S NOTE.
> *Jim had said on tape, that all along he had been told that she had double pneumonia. In fact, to have double pneumonia, infection in both lungs, you have to have two. Pearl only had one. If she knew she had only one, then she had been keeping him in the dark by saying she had double pneumonia. Was the single lung a part of the disability caused at birth and yet again a result of the supposed injuries caused to her mother whilst pregnant?*

I needed to ask my Dad for help to sort things out with my inability to read or write, but at the time he was very busy at work, being Christmas time and Boxing Day. I needed to ask my Dad to come with me to the Hospital because I didn't know what to do. I had never experienced this before, I was only twenty-three. To persuade him to come with me, I said to him

"I will give you some money to come with me, because I cannot understand all this and you have seen this before. You know what to do. I want you to come with me."

He said

"I can't come. I have to work and I will be losing money."

I said to him

"Just go to them and tell them you are taking time off to help your son who needs you to help him sort things out after the untimely death of his wife. He has no one else to turn to." To persuade him to come I said

"Take a week off work and I will pay you a week's wages. I need you there to help me out and that is what I want."

I wouldn't have suggested it, but I was in a pickle,

"I will really appreciate that. At the end of the month when I have got all this sorted, I will make sure you don't go short. Do that and you can help me sort things out"

So, he did do. We went to the hospital to get the Death Certificate, two days after Christmas. The people there knew what to do. It was complicated and really hard work for me, but with the help of my Dad, we got it all sorted there and went to the registry office to register the death. I hadn't got a clue what to do then.

I went back to the hospital to thank the Doctors because they had been very good to Pearl. I thanked them as much as I could. What else could I do, I had to carry on.

I thanked my Dad for the help and apologised for shouting at him about taking time off work. I said

"You should have known it would be very difficult for me. I had to shout at you when you were insisting that you had to go to work.

You know that I can't read or write and should have known that it was going to be difficult for me, very difficult. Why did I have to convince you that it would be difficult? I didn't enjoy doing the shouting. I shouldn't have needed to do that. Any way I will keep my promise to pay you."

From a friend at work, I discovered that my Dad would have got paid for a week off on compassionate leave in any case. In effect, my Dad got paid twice but didn't say anything.

When I found this out, I couldn't be bothered to tackle him about it. I had had enough by then.

I carried on regardless making arrangements with the Undertakers. We had discussed arrangements in the past and Pearl wanted to be buried in Irlam near her Mum.

We had to wait a while for there was a backlog with all the people who had died over the Christmas period, having died before Pearl. It was more than a week into the New Year before we could have the funeral. We had two cars to take everybody there. My Dad was a miserable bugger at the funeral.

After the funeral I had taken a week off work to sort things out. To get her personal things back from the hospital and sort her things out at home. I had to go and see her Aunties' in Irlam as they were to elderly to come down to our flat in Stretford for the funeral.

After everything settled down, I had to go back to work, but I felt ill. It was a reaction to what I had been doing which had caught up with me. The boss insisted that I took another fortnight off work to get myself right, it mattered because it gave me more time to come to terms with everything.

The people I worked for were very good and on many occasions, they helped me a lot. I got a lovely surprise when I went back to work; a big gift from all the workers. I started filling up, as you .do

We didn't have flowers at the funeral by request and asked people to donate money so that I could give it to charity. My fellow workers had taken a collection and I got nearly two hundred pounds. It was this that brought tears to my eyes.

I gave half of it to Cancer Research and the other half to the Heart Foundation. But now I had to get back to work.

I was very lonely, but life carries on when you to go back to work. It isn't easy but it made me realise how much I had loved Pearl. When it came to sorting through her personal things at home, that was something else that hit home.

I was going to give them to a clothing charity in Liverpool. I was very proud of myself for this was hard to do but I did it and everything was sorted.

To prevent myself from being lonely I threw myself into my work. I didn't feel like doing it but I was determined to stop myself from being lonely.

I lived at Railway Road for five years and continued to work for King Pin during that time. As usual for me, I was let go and I could no longer afford the rent so I had to go back to live with my Dad.

At that time, my sister and brother were still living at home. Sylvia the eldest sister and had a good education and had a very good job. She left home when she got married in 1969.

Peter, my brother would marry Pauline Hughes in 1973 and depart, leaving me and my youngest sister Patricia with my Dad and Mum.

I became restless after Pearls death and left King Pin three years after she died. I did not attempt to find a job, but eventually had to sign on at the Job Centre to get my dole money.

I did go out with a new girl, until I became ill. I was very poorly for a long time and lost my job. There were jobs I could have done but I was too ill. I always thought there must be someone worse than me.

When I was with Pearl, she was worse than me in many ways. I had always tried to help people, but someday I hoped someone would worry about me. It would have been nice for someone to think of me. That would have been a compliment.

When I recovered, I found a job in a company that dealt with Soya Beans where I stayed for four years.

Chapter Six

Life with My Dad

1960 – 2002

My first twenty years had seen an off and on relationship between my Dad and me. When I was twenty-one in November 1961, I was looking forward to a big party, even though Pearl could not be there.

But throughout my life I had never got birthday cards or presents as I was told that 22nd November was too close to Christmas to get gifts for both. This day would turn out just the same.

When Pearl was twenty-one, she got a card from her Dad who asked whether she wanted money or a present. She chose to have the money, which her Dad gave her.

I didn't get the alternative as I turned twenty-one, I didn't get anything. I didn't care; I was used to it. That was me and my Dad all over. That's the way things were. I couldn't think about what other people got. I had to leave it all behind.

I was lonely for a long time after Pearl had passed, then one day, the man who was the window cleaner became a friend. I really liked him and we became the best of friends. He said

"Come on you, you need to start going out and getting on with things." I said

"I will do eventually."

He said

"Never mind eventually, you are going out with me this weekend, so get yourself sorted.!"

He got me out of the rut and we would go to Salford, which was within easy walking distance, to enjoy a pub or a club, particularly the dockers club at Manchester docks at the end of the ship canal, which was still in use at that time.

On one occasion I tried to dance. Tried twelve of fifteen times. I said to myself you need to get some practice in, for it seemed I was messing about and about to have an accident.

Before I met Pearl, I went with a girl called Joan for about a year. She taught me to dance after a fashion and we did as much as we could.

At Christmas time we went to a club for Doctors and Nurses. They did a lot at Christmas time; Jim and his wife were there. They were a lovely couple. But I lost touch with them after that.

It wasn't long after that, when I had moved back to live with my Dad that he had a go at me again; subject normal. I had a go back, not violently, just told him what I thought.

I stayed in that night and he started boxing me. As I ducked to get out of the way, he gave me a good blow on my right ear. I ended up on the floor on my back, bruising it badly.

God, did that hurt. When I recovered, I said to him

"If you ever do that to me again, you will never do it again to anyone else."

He never did that to me again and good job and all. But I had to get my back sorted and my neck too.

I got another job working with good times. I did alright for a few years. I became a new version of Jim.

When I had been working with the Greyhounds a Belle Vue, I could hear the sound of motorbikes coming from the speedway track. I said to myself

"I am going to get a ticket for that one day!"

Little did I know that the speedway would form a major part of my life. in the future. In the meantime, my handicraft hobby was winning me prizes at the annual flower show that Dad entered with his flowers. He had a rivalry with another chap on the allotments.

After the years of loneliness, 1964 and 1965 I started to go to the speedway at Belle Vue. I went on a Sunday and became a fan of Belle Vue Aces following them around to various meetings. I was free to do this now. As you can imagine I was very busy.

It occupied most of my weekends and sometimes in the week as well. We went to away meetings all over the place, Halifax, Blackpool and even London. On the London trip we stayed for the weekend in a guest house.

As a result of this activity I was calming down, for we went to pubs and clubs for a few drinks. We were having a really good time. On one trip we went to the Speedway Finals at Wembley. We wanted a good laugh and along the way, I changed.

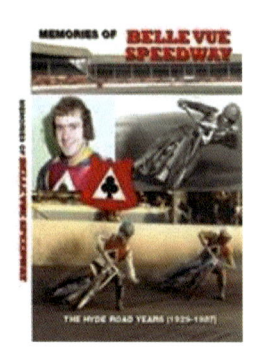

The girl who taught me to dance, was Joan, who I had dated before Pearl. We had fallen out when she did not like me talking to other girls. I said to her

"I am not your boyfriend. I am not a cushy number. I will talk to women if I want to and I like talking to women in the mornings. It is so easy to see things clearly in the morning. I will do this whether you like it or not!"

My Mum had told me to let her go!

But that is how I learned to dance.

Before I started going to the speedway, I went to the wrestling that Mum and Dad liked and where they met, in the 1930's. I went with a friend from work called Dick. We had another friend called Arthur; we all worked together.

After the wrestling we would go into Caesars Palace for a few drinks and in the end, we would go there on its own, as we had become bored with the wrestling.

The three of us, always together got the nickname of "The Three Wise Men" when on a trip following the Aces to Wimbledon.

I guy on that trip said did you know you had that nickname. You are always together, Go everywhere together, never apart. We had a good time; living it up.

Our trips to Caesars Palace had started the interest, because Dick decided he was going to get tickets for the Speedway the following weekend. It was easy to get them, for I already knew the girls in the ticket office from when I was working with the Greyhounds.

We were regulars for years and always sat in the same seats and so did a couple in front of us. They were called Les and Margaret. The three wise men would laugh and joke with them, having a good time.

Each of us had our favourite riders and we would have competitions between us. Plenty of friendly banter.

Margaret was shy at first but when we got to know them, she was alright. Of course, we did not see them between speedway seasons. However, Les invited me down for tea. He worked in Piccadilly Gardens, Central Manchester.

After we had our tea, Les went in the other room to watch the television, leaving Margaret and me alone. She started to tell me the troubles she was having in her marriage to Les. Apparently, she wanted to have children but Les was against it.

I realised I could become the pig in the middle, which I didn't want but I went down there over a period of two years. In the end I decided to stop going. Things were getting too serious, but I still saw them at Belle Vue.

During those two years, Margaret and I were often alone as Les would be at work, so you can imagine what he thought was going on! I did not want that to be thought and nothing was going on in any case. This was the reason I stopped going.

After that gap in my visits, I got a phone call from Les, could I come down. I thought that there was trouble there. I got on my bike and cycled all the way to Reddish where they lived. I thought maybe I could knock their heads together and solve the problem between them. When I got there, he didn't want to talk to me about his wife. I didn't solve any problems that night. I thought I could have been a mediator.

A few months later, I saw Les on the allotments with my Dad. They had been talking. After Les left I was collared by my Dad who proceeded to call me names.

"What had I been doing to cause Les to seek a divorce?

You must be a dirty little rat causing that split."

I wasn't having any of this, I was flaming mad. I called Margaret and told her that I was coming down to sort Les out, fight him. I felt like killing him as he had told my Dad that I was the cause of the split. I wasn't going to be his friend anymore if he carried on.

I went to their house after work. When I knocked on the door, Margaret opened it and Les was stood behind her smiling.

I took my coat off and was prepared to hit him but I couldn't do it. So, I said

"What were you doing with my Dad on the allotment? Why were you there and what did you say to him?

He had caused trouble with my Dad and I was blameless.

"You must have said something to upset him! After thinking about It at work, I have come here to smack you on the nose. I might still do it."

Margaret didn't know anything about this and he apologised after a fashion, smirking. Margaret was fuming, so I went home.

Back at home in the parlour, the phone rings and it is after ten at night. My Mum answered it and told me Margaret wanted to speak to me.

She was still angry and had called to offer another apology, which I accepted. I told her that if I hear anymore, I will come back and smack him this time. This upset my Mum once more.

A few weeks later, Margaret left Les and went back to live with her Mum, it was 1975. Her Mum lived in a high rise flat in the Hulme district. These had been built in the 1960's after all the slum terraced houses had been demolished.

Les was going to seek a divorce but Margaret beat him too it by seeing a solicitor first, and started the proceedings in 1975.

There was a court case for the divorce on the grounds of irreconcilable breakdown. Margaret got a financial settlement, 40% I think of their possessions.

I didn't see Les for a while at Belle Vue but eventually he came again. He had sold their house and Margaret had her settlement.

I would meet Margaret at her Mum's flat in 1976, a year before we got married.

What I didn't know was that Margaret had fell in love with me and we met every night after the divorce. In August 1977, on a park bench in Foley Park, I proposed, despite earlier, after Pearl's death, vowing never to get married again.

Editor' Note.

It had been rumoured that Les had an affair with a younger sister who became pregnant. It is not known whether the guilt involved, stopped him wanting a child with Margaret.

Les got married again two years after the divorce and had children.

We had to choose the Registry office, as no church would marry us as Margaret was divorced. My Dad didn't come to the wedding, it was not a popular idea with him.

In 1977, before the wedding, my Mum, came to the end of a prolonged illness which had started in 1975. The Doctors had discovered a cancer in her throat and had removed her voice box (larynx). She could only talk in grunts after that.

Her illness caused further trouble between me and my Dad as I was arranging everything for her. Sorting out the ambulances

My Mum had always told me that if ever she would be admitted to hospital long term, she would walk in but never walk out. After some time there, my Mum was scheduled to be transferred to a nursing home, but unfortunately, she died before that could happen in June 1997, two months before Margaret and I were due to get married.

Patricia and I had looked after her as much as we could while she was at home, but she had lung cancer as well as the initial throat problem. She had been a heavy smoker all her life. Mum didn't like visitors at the hospital, for she didn't want anyone to see her in her condition.

Sylvia was now living in Sale and had fallen out with Mum who thought she risen above her status. She had always been the princess of the family.

In 1973, when she was nineteen years old, my youngest sister Patricia was going with a lad who got her pregnant. She wanted to marry him but he did not want to get tied down so young.

When Dad found out he was angry enough for her to be asked to leave the household. Mum and I told him you can't do, she is pregnant and we must look after her.

He said well she should get an abortion. Patricia said

"No, I am going to have this child whether you like or not."

She had a little boy who she called Robert. He would grow up in the family and I liked him a lot. We got on very well.

He was a very bright lad, saving all his money in money

Patricia with Robert

boxes when he got them as presents and would often offer to lend me some to be returned with interest of course.

He had money for sweets, savings and some for a rainy day! My Dad even liked him!

After Patricia had Robert, she was going through a particularly bad time mentally and I would have long talks with her trying to help her solve her problems.

Patricia felt she had been left on the shelf, despite the fact that she had loads of boyfriends whom she could have married. She would run off and go missing for days. Got into taking drugs. I told her this had to stop and I didn't tell my Mum and Dad who weren't helping her in any way.

I think my Dad had taken a bad view of her after her pregnancy and the birth of Robert and they didn't get on.

I would counsel her and tell her that I had gone through a similar experience when I was younger, but she was lucky she had me to talk to about her troubles. All I had were the ducks who didn't help much.

This continued long after Margaret and I got married.

One night in 1979, I got a call from my Dad when Margaret and I were living in Ashover Street, so I wasn't very far from Lime Crescent. Could I come around immediately, something was wrong.

I went as quickly as I could, to be met by my Dad at the door who said

"The silly bitch has only gone done herself in!"

Dad and Patricia had not got on after the birth of Robert and when Mum died in 1977 and I was married they all three had to live together.

Apparently, what had happened was Dad was downstairs, Robert was asleep and Patricia was in her bedroom above the room where Dad was.

He had heard a rattling sound and then a crash onto the floor above. Running upstairs he found Patricia on the floor with a large gash on her head, and pills and pill bottles scattered all around.

She had taken an overdose of whatever pills they were and fallen gashing her head as she did it.

We had to call the police who initially thought my Dad had killed her with a blow to the head.

She had however, left letters addressed to several people and it was clearly a suicide. In one she said that her relationship with Dad was a factor that made her depressed.

I never understood why she hadn't come to me for I had been her confident for many years before. Why did she have to do it?

In another one of the letters she asked that Robert should not be left to be looked after by my Dad because of how he was with her. Robert was now six years old and she wanted him adopted.

Sylvia and Peter could not do that and as I will tell later neither did Margaret or I.

Robert was adopted by a wealthy couple who had a car business and he grew up to run his own business and children of his own. Once he was adopted, I lost contact with him and don't know where he lives.

He did tell me a few years later that he didn't want to come because I was always shouting at my Dad.

Dad continued to live on his own at Lime crescent until he was eighty in 1993. He had continued with his work for the corporation in the Parks until his retirement. He had continued with the flower shows he liked with flowers from his allotments

He then moved to Sale to be nearer to Sylvia, living in sheltered accommodation. Where he became ill and was placed in a nursing home.

I did what I could to help Sylvia, completing little jobs for her when I went to see my Dad. My wife Margaret used to say

"You are mad going there to help Sylvia."

I said

"But my Dad is there. He is still my Dad despite all that he has done!"

She said

"If that had been my Dad, I wouldn't want to let him know!"

I said

"That is your view. I still love him, whether he loves me or not. If he wants me to do things, I will do that!"

I couldn't not do them.

In 2002 he died of a heart attack at age 84. His health had never really recovered from the TB he had when younger.

Throughout his life I tried to get on with my Dad and make him proud of me.

I was proud of myself and tried many ways to get near to him. There was always this barrier and I couldn't get through it. I wanted him to say,

"Are you alright son? Are you doing alright?"

But he never did. I don't know why. I loved him so much but I couldn't get near to him.

I would go and see him on a Friday nad I continued to ask him why he didn't like me. He never said I love you even when I told him I loved him. I wondered sometimes if he ever loved me, but he never responded to that.

Chapter Seven

My Second Marriage

1977 -2013

I had known Margaret and her first husband Les for many years as we had met at the Belle Vue

Speedway. My friends and I, the three wise men had started going after Dick, one of our three bought tickets for a Sunday event.

We always sat in the same seats each time we went and Les and Margaret were in the row in front of us. Over time we got to know them both, although Margaret was a little shy at first.

We would have a lot of friendly banter as each of us had a favourite rider and we held competitions between ourselves as to whose rider would win a particular race.

We had been going to the Speedway for several years, although we did not see Margaret and Les in the closed season for Speedway. Margaret had invited me to their house in Reddish, which is near Belle Vue, to have some tea with them both.

I accepted her invitation and joined them for a meal. It was peculiar though for after tea, Les just got up and went in the other room to watch television, leaving Margaret and me alone.

We had a general conversation and then she began to tell me about all the troubles she had in her marriage. I could see that when Les had gone into the other room.

She told me that she would like to have a baby, but Les had always said no to this and it was a thorn in the marriage.

I had several invitations after that and must have visited several times. I realised I could become the pig in the middle, which I didn't want but I went down there over a period of two years. In the end I decided to stop going but I still saw them at Belle Vue.

Whilst I hadn't seen them for a while, Les called me on the phone, could I come down to the house now. I got on my bike and cycled all the way to Reddish where they lived, which was some distance from where I was living in Old Trafford.

When I arrived, Margaret was very upset. They must have had a big argument. I thought maybe I could knock their heads together and solve the problem between them. Les however, didn't want to talk about his wife as I tried solve the problems that night. I thought I could have been a mediator. It didn't work, but I stayed the whole weekend in my attempt.

A few months later, when I was passing my Dad's allotments, I saw Les with my Dad. They had been talking. Les had obviously been telling him all about the difficulties he and Margaret were having and blaming me for it. After Les left I was collared by my Dad who proceeded to call me names.

What had I been doing to cause Les to seek a divorce? What have you been doing with his wife? You must be a dirty little rat causing that split. I wasn't having any of this, I was completely innocent of any accusations.

As you can imagine my short temper flared up. I wasn't going to accept the story Les had told my Dad, who of course didn't believe me. It was typical of him and me.

I was flaming mad. I called Margaret and told her that I was coming down to sort Les out, fight him. I felt like killing him as he had told my Dad that I was the cause of the split. I wasn't going to be his friend anymore if he carried on.

A few weeks later, Margaret left Les and went back to live with her Mum in Hulme. There was a court case for the divorce on the grounds of irreconcilable breakdown. Margaret got a financial settlement, 40% I think of their possessions.

I used to go and see her at her Mums, but her Aunty who didn't live there, never liked me, even after I did a lot of work for her in her garden; she was a big woman. Her Dad had a heart attack when Margaret was eighteen and died at age sixty-four. He had been employed in the Highways department.

What I didn't know was when we met at Belle Vue for the Speedway, that Margaret had fell in love with me and we met every night after the divorce. She was six years younger than me having been born in 1946.

In August 1977, on a park bench in Foley Park, I proposed, despite earlier, after Pearl's death, vowing "never" to get married again. We had a quiet wedding at the registry office in Manchester and had to find some where to live.

The reception was held back at Lime Crescent. Ted a friend from work, a very tall man, was my best Man. Sylvia who didn't come to the wedding was at the reception.

The guests all line up outside the house for photographs.

For about six months after the wedding we lived apart, me with Dad and Margaret with her Mum and Aunty, who had moved in after the death of her husband.

Margaret had said that she was going to buy a house with the money she had got from the divorce and even though we were married we were still living apart, Margaret at her Mums in Hulme and me in Old Trafford.

I didn't think I could afford to

Margaret, her Aunty in pale blue and Mum to her left

buy a house but a mate at work

"Why don't you get a mortgage?"

This was all new to me but he told me to go and see the bank manager.

Margaret arranged an appointment with the Royal Bank of Scotland and we met a manager there. He was a very nice man and very helpful.

We discussed our situation. I was working and Margaret too, He took down all our details and said we had the qualifications for a mortgage. But I said

"We don't have an account here." He

replied

"That is not a problem just open an account put some money in it, five pound will do."

I think between us we found fifty pounds to deposit in the account there and then and we got a mortgage. I had a bit of money saved and Margaret had the settlement from the sale of her former house in Reddish. We put this all together to reduce the amount borrowed.

We borrowed £12500 and the bank manager said we could have a bigger loan if we wanted, but we were happy with that amount. We were able to pay this off over twelve years.

When we moved in, I couldn't afford a lawn mower, but over the years I did a lot of work in the garden. I had been working for Manchester Corporation as a gardener, before that in an engineering company in Old Trafford, near the Barton Bridge. I left the gardening job. I got fed up of travelling all-round the city to do the gardens.

My Dad of course said I was stupid buying a house. Same old broken record. He said I was not old enough, at 27? This made me more determined than ever to get a house.

We found a house in Stretford, just around the corner from where I worked. We paid twelve thousand eight hundred and fifty pounds for the house. At the time I was working for Forest City Signs, my brother worked there too. I didn't have much to do with him because I had lost contact when I was with Pearl.

In any case he worked in a different department in another building where he was designing the signs for motorways and other roads.

I worked alongside a welder who was making metal bollards. My job was to smooth off the welds before they were painted.

I hadn't been working there very long, but was settling down into the job when we went holiday. It was a delayed honeymoon in the Cotswolds. We were away for a week.

We came back mid-week and I went to work the following day. When I got to the factory it was all locked up. Nobody was there. I asked around as to what was going but nobody seemed to know.

It took me three weeks to discover where the company had moved to. When I did, I went there and went to the boss and said nobody told me you were moving.

He said he hadn't told me because we were going on holiday and he didn't want to spoil that. I said "It has taken me three weeks to find out where you had gone too and I have lost all my wages from those three weeks." He replied

"I think we will be alright Jim, I can find you a new job."

"As it was my fault in not telling you, I will pay you the lost wages, but as it is Thursday, take the rest of the week off and come to work on Monday." Which I did.

The manager of the company understood the problem and it would be good to see Jim at work. I said

"You know I always work hard, and I will continue to work hard for you."

He explained the new job, and I got all written down with the agreed wage payments, which were alright with me.

I said

"You know I will volunteer for any extra work and I will turn up for work on time. You know I am well mannered."

I was glad to get home that night to Margaret. She wasn't happy about the situation and didn't say much, just sat there. We didn't talk much about whether this was the right decision.

My Dad didn't like Margaret but Mum got on very well with her until she died. We had this house in Stretford, 33 Ashover St.

It was 1978. We would be married a long time, thirty-six years.

We got to know the neighbours and had a lot of social activities with them. The little girl in the picture is called Michelle. One day she announced to her parents that I was her second Dad for we had a special relationship.

That connection was to last all my life. She stayed friendly with Margaret and me even after she was married. She was and still is fascinated by the Disney characters, her childhood obsession, even as an adult.

It wasn't long before I fell back on hard times. I was made redundant and got half a week's pay for each year I had been there. I would be out of work for five years. Shortly after, Margaret was made redundant too. She worked for a company making wallpaper. She got more than me, a full week's wages for each year.

We had to live on Dole money and we were very short at times. Margaret eventually got a job, which she didn't like, working for an industrial cleaning company in Old Trafford.

We had always done very well from that wallpaper company and had stacks of wallpaper at home. I had never hung wallpaper before but as my Dad was a painter and decorator, I had watched him many times.

So, I set too, pasting the paper, folding like he did as well as I could and placed on the wall. I thought I made a very good job of it.
Dad came around and looked at it said

"Well son, you have made a very good job of that. I can't see the seams, but there is one problem."

Me being proud of what I had achieved said

"What problem?"

He said

"You have put it on upside down!"

I had to set too and remove each strip and hang it up the other way.

Of course, I tried very, very hard to get a job but it was difficult. I was always honest at interviews telling them about my limited education but that did not help much. I knew we couldn't live like this.

I did find odd jobs during that time, enough to get coal in and keep us warm at weekends. I was always at the Job Centre a 9 o'clock in the morning, even before they opened.

They saw me alright there of course, everybody seemed to like me. Why, I don't know but they did. I tried very hard to get a job with so many interviews I had.

I used walk and cycle all over the place to find a job. People would write letters for me to help with the search.

I got some answers from firms, but when it came to the interview, I was honest about my lack of education. I didn't want to tell lies in case they found out.

I used to tell them the truth, but as you can imagine, it didn't help much; didn't help at all really. Looking back, it was silly of me to do that.

Anyway, I carried on regardless in the hope that one day I would get a job. It didn't happen.

Eventually a friend also called Jim, called me and said you had better go back to the job centre for they have jobs there. I am going, come with me.

I hadn't seen Jim for ten years and we had been good friends but so much had changed in those years. When we got there, it was like charity morning. I hadn't seen anything like it there before. Companies were advertising all sorts of jobs. It was early 1996.

He was a very good friend to me, much more than I could be to him. He carried me. I said

"Listen, I have been going to the Job Centre for five years now and couldn't get a job. What chance have I got of getting a job now. There are no jobs going for me!"

He said

"I have been on the sick but I work here now. I am not going to make it easy for you." I said

"You are very fortunate because of your schooling and you can do well at that. I didn't have that in my young life, but good on you."

Previously, I spoke to a man at the Stretford Job Centre and he asked me how old I was. I said

"I am fifty-four, but for twelve of those years, I have been out of work. I have been trying so very hard to get a job."

I told him the truth, saying

"I can't remember how many enquiries I put out but didn't get anything for five years and that was five years for hard work put in looking for jobs." I couldn't think that things would change for me. I tried moving on, not worrying, keeping chirpy. I always got a letter saying I was not suitable. It was very degrading.

The next time I went down to the Job Centre, it was the very first time I had gone and expressed my anger and disappointment. I said to the young lady

"Don't take this to heart, it is not personal but I am not having this! Here is my card and you won't see me again. I have had enough. I can't be doing with this anymore. I know I am not working, but I don't give a monkeys this time." And I left.

About three months later, I had been out looking for work and when I got home, Margaret said to me that Jim had been on the phone and I should go back for they wanted to see me. I said "I am not going back there, I don't want to know. They can do what they want!

She said

"Listen! You have to go, they want to see you. You had better go!

I went back and saw Jim. He said

"I have got you an interview with a chap. He is in that room. He has come from Marks and Spencer's. He is a very nice chap. You will find him interesting." I thought yeah, yeah and wasn't convinced. Nevertheless, I went in to meet him and he was a very nice chap as Jim had said. He was very understanding.

I was in there for over half an hour and we had a wide-ranging talk. The interview was for a job in Marks and Spencer's store in City Centre Manchester, on the corner of Cross Street and Market Street.

At the end of the interview, he said

"I like you. You are very smart, very nicely dressed and I like what I see. I like your honesty about everything and I believe you are very clever."

This was the first time I had ever been told that and couldn't accept it. I said

"If I was clever, I wouldn't be out of work for so long!"

He disagreed.

"No, you are very smart and you presented yourself very well to me. You are open and honest and that is what I like about you."

"I am going to put you down to have another interview unfortunately this necessary. This will be in the store in the City Centre."

"I am here to gather as many people as I can, I am looking for six, and you will be one of them. I have you on my list"

In the meantime, he advised me to continue looking for jobs, for if you present yourself as you did to me today, then getting a job should not be a problem.

"You are very smart and present yourself well. I like your attitude."

Little did he know that I had stuffed cardboard in my shoes to cover the holes.

I said

"I do try and that's my problem. I think I try too hard sometimes but you can't be blamed for trying, can you? He said

"Very well just keep coming, for I believe you haven't been coming for three months." I said

pg. 121

"No, I haven't. I had had enough of all the rejections and I was fed up." He said

"Well you have this interview coming up but you must keep coming here. You never know you might get lucky. Keep trying and you will be hearing from them."

I did go for a few more jobs. I didn't get any of them. It was not for the want of trying. Then I got the letter for my interview in town. I brushed off my suit, replaced the cardboard in my shoes and went for the interview. I was so polite again as I was interviewed by a lady this time. She said to me

"I like what I see."

I was there all day and got a midday meal paid for and bus fare too. After the meal, I had to try a few things that would be involved with the job.

They told me how many persons were working on each floor. How many security guards there were: four on each floor.

I said

"Well, won't be troubling any of them!"

Two weeks later, I got a letter asking me to go back. I saw her again and she told me I had got the job. I stood there for a while, almost in a trance. I was not used to working for a big company. It was all new to me.

Despite all the hard times I always seemed to come out on top eventually.

I loved the job and I had been working there for eight weeks when on one Saturday, June the 15th

1996, I got off the bus in Piccadilly Bus station and was making my way towards the top end of Market Street, which I had to walk down to get to the store.

This is the lorry containing the bomb, the biggest bomb to have ever been planted by the provisional IRA

There was a big crowd there and the Police were holding them back. Market Street was closed. The Police told us there was a bomb scare and we couldn't go down. We were waiting for about two hours,

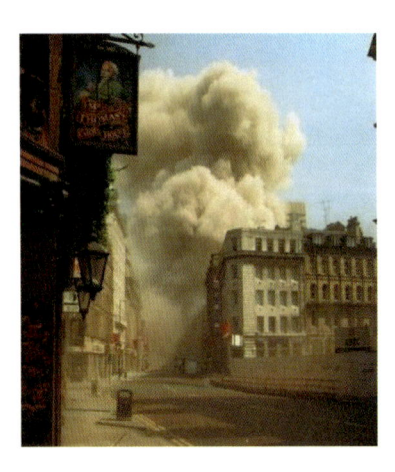

I was with a guy who worked alongside of me at Marks and Spencer.

He said

"We shall be alright because of the hotel there. They are not going to bomb that!"

pg. 124

Suddenly, there was a terrific explosion. Smoke and dust everywhere. Some people were hit by flying glass although most of the 80,000 people there had been evacuated in time. The Police told us the bomb was outside Marks and Spencer's.

I thought

"Here we go again."

I have just started and here goes my job. Unemployed again. I got on a bus and went home.

Everybody who worked in the store were safe and I don't think anyone was killed for there had been sufficient warning. It was an IRA bomb.

All the employees were contacted and told to attend a meeting the following week. There, we were told that we wouldn't lose any wages and our jobs were secure. They were going to find places in alternative M&S stores for all of us.

I knew what I was going to do. I went to the store in Ashton-under-Lyne and got my job there, doing the same job as I had been offered in the City centre store. I worked there until my retirement in 2000.

When I look back on all the interviews, I had and the questions I was asked, I have to laugh.

One time, I was offered a job working on the Corporation tip but I needed O-levels or GCSE exam results and a driving licence.

They had to be kidding didn't they. It really annoyed me and many a time I was told I was too old at forty-five. Talk about age discrimination! I covered miles searching for jobs which caused the hole in my shoe. We didn't have enough money to get it repaired.

Working in Ashton-under-Lyne, it was a fair distance from our house in Stretford, so we decided to move and bought a house in Droyslden. With the increase in value of our first house, we were even able to reduce our mortgage. This house was only one bus away from the store.

When we had money, we enjoyed a summer holiday and many times we went to Devon, eleven years in total, staying in a little cottage just outside the fishing village of Brixham. Summer days in the sun away from the big city. Very relaxing and all too short.

I still followed the speedway and there was a trip organised to go to the World Championships in Gothenburg, Sweden. My mate Ted who had been my best man said why don't you go.

I of course couldn't afford it at the time and I told him. He said

"Listen, I will lend you the money and you can pay it me back whenever you can."

He gave me £250 so I booked the trip. Margaret encouraged me to go too. We went by coach, on a ferry to Holland and then by road to Gothenburg.

It was a very enjoyable weekend and new experiences with border crossings and passport checks.

I was amazed at the size of the streets, compared to Manchester. We stayed in a hotel and me, not being used to foreign lands didn't know what a continental breakfast was. When the pastries arrived, I said

"Is that it? I can't survive on that I need a proper breakfast!"

We decided to walk out in search of "proper food". All we could find was a street seller with bananas. I bought a large bag, enough for all my meals at the weekend and some left for the coach trip home.

I paid back the £250 in six weeks.

Although one of the reasons Margaret had left Les was because she wanted a child and he did not, we did not have any children. Margaret had made a stance saying

"I am not bringing up children on the social."

By this of course she meant the dole money we were receiving as I didn't have a job for twelve years.

After Patricia's suicide, the question of Robert's adoption came up. I had a good relationship with the little lad and would dearly have liked to take him on. He was now six years old, a fact that put Margaret off. She said she would have adopted him had he been a baby but she was not prepared to take over at six. Sylvia and Peter were not interested either.

In December 2000, Margaret's Mum died after a fall in her flat in Hulme. She was 74. She had been living there with Margaret's Aunty, Mrs Moss.

Why do deaths always happen to me at Christmas time?

Two months later, her Aunt Mrs Moss fell down the stairs. Neighbours tried to pick her up but couldn't do that, she was a big woman. She died as a result of this fall. She had been related to Margaret's Mum by marriage to a husband with whom she led a dog's life.

Her husband had been Margaret's Mum's brother and her Aunt blamed Margaret's Mum for the life he had. I never liked her Aunt.

Margaret's Dad had died of a heart attack when she was young and I never knew him. He was only 54.

I worked at Marks and Spencer until my retirement. Margaret and me were happy living in Droylsden, but there was something wrong with her health.

Margaret didn't like Doctors and was very reluctant to go, but when I finally got her there, the blood tests she had proved nothing.

The Doctor said she was alright but this weakness went on for two years. I got to the point where she was having difficulty getting upstairs.

I brought her bed down and made a bedroom for her on the ground floor so that she did not have to climb the stairs and get so out of breath.

I would find her lying in bed, doubled in pain, but still she did not want to go to the Doctor. After a while sleeping there, she said she wanted to go back upstairs and set off on the climb.

Halfway up, she came to a complete standstill and couldn't move. I had to get her down. I lifted her in a fireman's lift, not easy as she had put on weight, and brought back to the bed.

It wasn't right. I called Sylvia asking what to do now. She said call an ambulance, which I did and Margaret was taken to Tameside Hospital

She was seen by the Doctors at the hospital who took me aside and told me that she had cancer. Cancer of the lung.

I wasn't surprised for she had been a heavy smoker all her life. I smoked too at that time. I went back to her bedside and told her that I was giving up smoking there and then.

She laughed saying you won't be able to keep that up! You will be back on them within a week.

I had a very bad cough and the news about Margaret made be determined and I never smoked again.

The Doctor said that Margaret's cancer was very bad and he didn't give her much hope of surviving.

A week later, on a weekend, in the early hours of the morning she died. As she had only been there a short while it was necessary for there to be a post mortem examination, which was carried out on the Monday.

Yet again, the past recurred. Like with Pearl, the funeral was delayed by holiday times. She had died on the 16th July 2013.

This time I organised it, with the help of Sylvia. I thought she was very good for doing that with me.

Her experience with my Dad's funeral came in handy.

I asked that no flowers be sent, as I did for Pearl, and all donations of money I gave to the Macmillan nurses. There was £400 but I called them to say, that they would have to send someone to collect it as I was in no fit state to take it to them.

I did that because I appreciated the work that they do and the comfort I had received from them during the last days of Margaret's illness.

Chapter Eight

Alone Again

2013 –

I lived alone in that house for a month and then I got ill too. I was taken into hospital and had an operation on my stomach. They removed part of my bowel and I had to have a bag on my left-hand side.

I was very weak and my sister wanted me to come a stay with her for a while. By this time Sylvia had moved to a small village in South Cheshire called Audlem.

It needed a second operation to reverse the connection to my bowel. I was very weak after this and I went to stay in a nursing home called Corbrook, which was only about a mile from Audlem. All in all, I had been in hospital for 7 months. The Macmillan nurses used to visit me at Corbrook.

I was there when I had a sudden pain in my chest and I collapsed. When I woke up I didn't no where I was, but there were nurses there.

I was able to talk and ask them where I was. They told me that I was in the intensive care unit at the hospital, for I had had a heart attack.

I asked

"what time is it?"

The nurse said

"12 o'clock."

Thinking it was 12 midday I asked her to call my sister and tell her where I am. She said

"I can't do that now."

I didn't understand until she told me it was the middle of the night and "bang" I had another heart attack.

This time I woke up in a dark room and Sylvia was there sitting in a chair. I didn't know what had happened.

She said

Oh, your back!"

Corbrook Park

I was in that hospital for some time and discharged back to the nursing home. Sylvia visited me one day, and told me that I didn't have to worry about the house in Droylsden as she and her husband had sold it for me, and they had found a place in a town called Nantwich where I could live.

Nantwich was only six miles from Audlem and they had found me a ground floor flat in a block which had been constructed by McCarthy and Stone in 2002, specialists in residential property for the elderly. With the money from my house sale I could by this.

It was an apartment block for over 55's, Wright Court, and I could get carers there to help me. I moved in and as I had restricted movement, the carers came for 6 months.

By the seventh month I had recovered sufficiently to dispense with the carers and do it all myself with the help of a cleaner.

When I did this, Sylvia said to me

"You are very bright. You have done very well in Wright Court even though you can't read or write."

In all those years we had not been in contact, she did not know the half of it. She didn't really know me until then.

I didn't know anyone there at Wright Court and as I hadn't been out of my flat for seven months, no one knew me.

Eventually I got to know the residents from meeting them in the communal laundry and in the resident's lounge. We had social occasions, one of which was a coach trip to the Severn Valley railway at Bridgnorth.

I live there now and Sylvia does many things to help me. I still walk with a stick and have a mobility scooter which Sylvia arranged for me. I can use this to go into the town centre, weather permitting.

Sylvia and her husband will take me out occasionally to any hospital or doctors' appointments I need, as I have a car on the Motability scheme which they can drive.

I have lost close contact with my brother. He has only been here twice in six years although we do regularly speak on the telephone.

He had been a Teddy boy in his youth complete with drape suit, hairstyle and shoes. Running with gangs.

He still lives in Stretford, Manchester. Although we shared a bedroom when I went back to live my Mum and Dad after Pearls death, he got married to Pauline and moved away.

My visitor closest to me, apart from Sylvia, is Michelle who is like a daughter to me and visits often. She has been this way ever since those days back in Ashover Street in Stretford.

I have many friends in the apartment block, one of whom, Trevor has been close to me from the beginning. Trevor's wife, Pat, is a collector of handbags and will regularly offer one to Michelle, including one complete with Disney characters. You can imagine how much Michelle loved it.

I became friendly with Rob about two years ago when he moved into a flat down the corridor from me. He very kindly helped me to construct this book.

James (Jim) Du Pre Deal
1940 -

Printed in Great Britain
by Amazon